ALSO BY CARL DENNIS

POETRY

A House of My Own

Climbing Down

Signs and Wonders

The Near World

The Outskirts of Troy

Meetings with Time

Ranking the Wishes

Practical Gods

New and Selected Poems 1974–2004

Unknown Friends

Callings

Another Reason

Night School

PROSE

Poetry as Persuasion

EARTHBORN

EARTHBORN

Carl Dennis

PENGUIN POETS

PENGUIN BOOKS

An imprint of Penguin Random House LLC
penguinrandomhouse.com

LIBRARY OF CONGRESS CATALOGING-IN-PUBLICATION DATA
Names: Dennis, Carl, author.
Title: Earthborn / Carl Dennis.
Description: [New York]: Penguin Books, an imprint of Penguin Random House
LLC, [2022] | Series: Penguin poets
Identifiers: LCCN 2021022957 (print) | LCCN 2021022958 (ebook) |
ISBN 9780143137016 (paperback) | ISBN 9780525508533 (ebook)
Subjects: LCGFT: Poetry.
Classification: LCC PS3554.E535 E27 2022 (print) |
LCC PS3554.E535 (ebook) | DDC 811/.54—dc23
LC record available at https://lccn.loc.gov/2021022957
LC ebook record available at https://lccn.loc.gov/2021022958

Printed in the United States of America
1st Printing

Set in Garamond 3 LT Pro
Designed by Sabrina Bowers

To the memory of Tony Hoagland,

for all he has left us

Acknowledgments

Thanks are due to the editors of the following magazines in which some of these poems first appeared:

The Cincinnati Review ("A Romance")

Colorado Review ("Children's Day" and "The Fall of Man")

Five Points ("Primitive")

The Florida Review ("A Daughter of the Puritans" and "Down Here")

Interim ("Three Pages")

The Nation ("Second Best")

New England Review ("At Chartres")

New Letters ("Too Bad" and "War and Peace")

The New Yorker ("Bottle of Wine" and "Former Lives")

Salmagundi ("Dependence Day" and "Sunday with Trees")

Seneca Review ("The Right Time")

This manuscript has benefited greatly from careful readings by several critical friends: Charles Altieri, Thomas Centolella, Alan Feldman, Mark Halliday, Philip Schultz, and Emily Wheeler.
"Dependence Day" is for Thomas Centolella.
"Simon Pell" is for Alan Feldman.
"In Traffic" is for Philip Schultz.

Contents

I

II

III

IV

V

VI

EARTHBORN

I

Canadian Hemlock

Nothing is improved by being praised.
But that doesn't mean the bestowing of praise
On whatever deserves it isn't a useful calling
Even if no one is listening at the moment,
If I'm alone now on my morning walk,
Waiting at the corner of Bryant and Richmond
For the light to change, open to the company
Of this stunted hemlock on the strip of grass
Between sidewalk and curb. A gnarled hemlock
Barely five feet tall, which I must have passed
A thousand times without remarking,
And may forget to observe in the future.
So this seems the moment to note that whatever
Fungus or parasite has besieged it has failed
To thwart its efforts to continue.
I don't want to claim too much, to project
Emotions upon it that it doesn't feel.
But I don't want to praise too little, to deny
It possesses the green equivalent of fortitude
For fighting an invader to a standstill,
Just as I wouldn't want to limit my motive
For taking my morning walk to a need for exercise.
I want to be one of the witnesses of the familiar
Open to revelation but not disposed
To insist on it. Let the tree withhold
What it wants to withhold. Let me see
What I'm ready to see now
When I set aside the notion that more is coming,
More reserved for some other day.

Bottle of Wine

I like to park a few blocks from the house of my hosts
And walk with my bottle of wine the tree-lined streets,
Anticipating the dinner with friends that awaits me.
A bottle of wine showing not only that I'm grateful
To be included but that I'm eager to do my part,
To offer a gift that won't survive the evening,
That says I've set aside the need for transcendence
And made my peace at last with living in time.
Soon we'll welcome the evening with a toast.
Soon we'll be toasting it in farewell
As it starts on its journey into the near past
And then the far. Do the houses I'm passing
Regard me as a creature about to vanish
Into the realm of shadow while they have resolved
To hold their ground? But the bottle I'm carrying
Shows how the past can enhance the present.
The grapes it was made from were plucked and pressed
Seven years ago in a vineyard in Burgundy
According to customs already in place for generations
By the time these houses moved from the realm
Of blueprints and estimates into brick and wood.
The bottle will testify that traditions once honored
Are being adhered to still, with patience, with pride.
And if the past is present this evening, isn't the future
Present as well in the thought that the ritual
I'm helping to pass along may prove enduring,
That however much the world around it alters,
Guests may still perform it in eras to come?
I hope I feel their presence in spirit
Under these trees later this evening
As I walk back to my car with empty hands.

Primitive

It wasn't a conviction that life is holy
That kept me from drowning the spider I found
In the sink this morning, that caused me instead
To cover it with a cup, slide a postcard beneath it,
And carry it out to the patio. It was more
The thought that it seemed unfair to kill it
Merely because it had wandered into my house.
But does the concept of fairness apply
To a creature that feeds without qualms
On insects that fail to notice its web in time?
A creature too dependent on instinct to profit
From my pointed example of self-restraint,
However often I repeat it.
Maybe it makes more sense to confess
To the fear I inherited from my earliest ancestors
Of arousing the wrath of the goddess of spiders
By harming one of her little spinners.
And if I'm not superstitious, what about the fear
That if I deem a spider dispensable I might
Come to think the same about higher life-forms?
I can't put it past me: wanting to draw up a list
Of the people whose absence would make the world
Far friendlier than it is, and then
Wanting to pass my list around.

Guest List

When it comes to the perfect guest for dinner,
I can't think of anyone like my late friend Martin,
Who showed how lucky he felt to be invited
Not by murmuring compliments
But by eating two helpings of every dish,
Indifferent to whether or not the other guests
Assumed he had trouble controlling his appetite.

And when the talk veered close to gossip,
I could count on him to break in with a long,
Vivid description of his latest dream, a jumble of scenes
He needed help arranging. It didn't matter to him
If others assumed he craved attention,
If they failed to notice how relieved he was
When somebody else broke in with a dream
That seemed more coherent and consequential.

And if somebody wanted to share with the company
A long account of her stroll the evening before
From her house in town to the reservoir,
However uneventful, Martin would ask for more details.
That sounds like the kind of walk he'd prefer any day,
He'd assure her, a walk to see what the dusk might offer,
As opposed to brooding alone in his room.

And when another guest admitted he'd napped
For much of the afternoon in his hammock,
Though his lawn needed raking and weeding,
Martin was quick to defend him against the charge
Of idleness. No better way to welcome the sun

Back from its absence of many days
Than by devoting an afternoon to basking.

Good for you, brother, Martin would say,
For not taking the sun's return for granted.
Whatever tomorrow asks of you,
Today is a red-letter day on the calendar
When the usual chores must be set aside.

Another Earth Day

No questions asked of those who gather today
To clear trash from the creek that winds through town,
So you needn't worry that if you join us
You'll be joining an assembly of the smugly righteous.
Some may be here because they're concerned
About the harm that the trash may do to the value
Of their creek-side property, and some because
A friend of theirs asked for their company.
And if these are free from the vice of littering,
Others may have come today to atone.
Maybe the young man struggling to pull a tire
To shore was the boy who threw the stone,
Two years ago, that shattered the streetlamp
Across from your house, a gesture meant
To convince the boys he ran with that the law,
Though it cowed most people, didn't cow him.
The teenage girl gathering cans and bottles
May have tried her hardest to scratch the mirror
In the girls' bathroom at Mercy High School
As an act of protest against the face
It claimed to be hers. And the veteran whose pile
Includes a shopping cart and a TV screen
May be doing his best, for all we know,
To appease his conscience for dropping his cigarette
On a handwoven rug in a house in Kandahar
And grinding it out with his heel to show the owners
How angry he was for their meager cooperation.
You can think of their piles as acts of penance
Offered the goddess assigned to protect the creek,
Whose capacity for forgiveness is proverbial,
Who will gladly read your willingness to join the cleanup,

If you want her to, as more than sufficient evidence
Of true contrition. Any disturbance of spirit that once
May have shown itself in your need to mar things
Is now behind you, she's certain.
And those in doubt can watch you work.

Winter Gift

Once the seasons were gods, immortal beings
Whose decisions were final. It was up to us
To bring our schedules in line with theirs:
To plant in spring, harvest in fall,
And then spend weekends splitting and stacking
Cords of hardwood that we hoped would last us
To the end of winter. Now the seasons
Seem to be wards of the state, like bison.

Gone the era when a week like this one,
Balmy and bright in mid-December,
Would have been regarded by all—
Except for a few sick with suspicion—
As a gift. Now it seems right to ask
If winter, though barely begun, is spent,
So hesitant it appears, so frail.

Once, those who scouted in March
For the blooms of the first ephemerals
Could expect to be disappointed. Now
They're successful, and the news is sobering.
Who knows how many generations
Will have to pass, in the best scenario,
Before Thoreau's notations on early blooming
In the woods near Walden are again reliable?

Eden for them will be a spring
That's willing to wait its turn while winter
Takes its own good time about departing.
What joy when the earliest trillium,
Earliest trout lily or bluebell,

Appears at last to those who have learned
How to look for a lone example,
One fleck of color in a field of snow.

From the Trustees of Forest Lawn

This is your yearly reminder that Forest Lawn
Isn't only a shady retreat in the middle of town
For strolling and musing. It's also a beautiful
Resting place for what will be left of you
When your spirit vanishes. Yes, a decade or more
May still be yours if your health is better than average,
But accidents happen. It isn't too early
To decide on the individual plot that seems,
Among our many bosky acres, especially restful,
Not if you want to spare your friends and family
The burden of making a choice in haste and grief
That ought to be made in tranquility. When they visit,
In a time not distant, leaning on canes and walkers,
Think how relieved they'll feel that you've chosen
A spot not far from the path, how grateful
For the marble bench we suggest you provide
For them to rest on while they ponder the part
You played in their histories, though they realize
There was much about you they never knew.
As for the good you'll be doing yourself this moment
By choosing your grave site now, consider how different
A day is going to look once you acknowledge
That your extinction is more than a probability,
That this day is one of the numbered few remaining,
One of the little cups that will have to hold
The pressings of all the grapes you pluck.
Sign a contract with us, and the town
You may have considered only a rest stop
Will reveal itself as your final sphere of action.
Think how much closer you'll feel to your acquaintances
When you decide to bestow on them

All the insights you may have been saving
For unknown others. It's time to be like the tree
That we suggest you invest in to shade your bench.
Every spring it will shower its seeds
On the soil around it without once asking
Whether or not the soil deserves them,
Seeds that will work with what they find.

Down Here

The most useful item brought back from the moon
Isn't one of the moon rocks but the photograph
Of an earthrise, the beautiful, blue-green globe
Floating alone in a black sky.
Those who look at it every morning are likely
To wish that Earth Day came more often
And enticed more people to join the cleanup.

Does the photograph tell us to cancel funding
For more space exploration? No, it merely suggests
We need to treat our home with the consideration
That it deserves before we assume that other
Inhabitants of the Milky Way
Will want to welcome us to their neighborhood.

Meanwhile an Earth Day pamphlet may suggest,
If we'd like a fresh perspective, that we turn
To the tall tree in our own backyard
And climb the ladder we lean against it
Up to the lookout. From there, it's not hard
To imagine looking down from a perch still higher
On a house and yard grown small and frail.

What if our homestead, the pamphlet asks,
Isn't the dead weight we sometimes feel
Stooping our shoulders, if it's more
A loose assembly of matchsticks and moss
That the first strong gust may sweep away?

From high in the tree, the white sheets
Drying on the line with our other laundry—

Shirts and blouses, pajamas and underwear—
Flutter like tiny prayer flags,
Petitioning us to join them on the ground.

II

Stoplight

On other nights you may be right to assume
That the only car waiting at the stoplight
In a one-light town at two in the morning
When you blow past it is driven by someone
Who's a slave to rules, or to the fear
He's being photographed by a hidden camera.
But tonight the driver could be my friend Sebastian,
A man in no hurry to go somewhere.

If he glimpses your car as you flash by,
He may simply assume you're young,
Speeding all night to spend a day with a woman
You wish you could see more often.

That's just what he did when he was young,
Drove fast for hours for a one-day visit
With the woman he later married,
Whose death just a month ago explains,
If you're interested, why he's out driving
At two in the morning, why he'd like
To postpone for a while his return
To a house that's silent.

And if, when the light turns green,
He turns his car in the direction of home,
It won't mean he's ready to begin the five-step journey
From grief to recovery that many
Now in their beds have recommended,
People you might agree with.
It will mean he would rather linger

Where his wife's absence is palpable
Than look for a place devoid of memories.

I hope your hurry means that someone
You're longing to visit expects to see you
This very morning, not that you're anxious
To put the past behind you, to get away.

A Hat

Being old may mean that I don't have time now
For withholding judgment till I have more facts.
It's now or never to fill in the gaps with the work
Of imagining, to resist my first reaction
When I get to the bus stop on finding a tall,
Stout, middle-aged woman wearing a huge
Straw hat with a fillet of cloth daisies
Draped round the brim. Instead of regarding the hat
As a pathetic attempt at a striking style,
I might ask myself if a hat like this one
Was a fad for a while among the girls
At her town's one school. If it was,
Then wearing one now may not be a fashion statement
So much as a gesture of solidarity with an era
Long gone, or with a particular friend
Who dreamed up the original just to be outlandish,
To thumb her nose at village blandness,
Village proprieties. When a girl, this woman
May have lacked the courage to follow
Her friend's example, but now she has it.
Why should she care that the stiff-necked old man
Who's just arrived at the bus stop
Gives her what seems a glance of pinched dismissal
And doesn't look back again to nod a greeting?
Let him think what he wants to think
While she's true to her deepest wish:
The wish that her friend could see her now.

In Traffic

Once I master the art of meditation,
I won't be one of the drivers stalled in traffic like this
Who lean on their horns. I'll accept the waiting
As a lucky spell of quiet for musing on questions
I've been neglecting, like whether my life is full
Or empty, and if empty, how best to fill it.
And if full, what's the best way to demonstrate
I appreciate my good fortune, including the dinner
With friends that I may be a little late for.
Yes, if they hadn't moved to the suburbs
After thirty years in a house five blocks from mine,
I'd have been there more than an hour ago.
But that's the kind of thought I'll set behind me
When I learn to meditate on human variety
And the many good reasons for embracing change.
And instead of blaming this traffic jam
On the broken stoplight I can now see flickering
Mindlessly up ahead, and blaming whoever's responsible
For keeping the lights in repair, I'll reflect awhile
On all I owe the lights when they're working
And all I owe to their little-known inventor.
I'll hope it earned him, or her, a decent income,
Though I'll still be moved by the arguments Franklin used
To explain why he sought no patents for his stove
Or his lightning rod, his sense that he borrowed
Most of his notions from the general fund
Of human knowledge accrued over centuries.
Any teachers of meditation who claim their methods
Are their own discoveries won't interest me.
I'll seek out those who think of themselves
As channels for the teachings of long ago,

Including advice for novices caught in traffic
About climbing above the dinner it now appears
I'll be missing completely. Does my absence
Hang like a heavy pall on the company?
Isn't a question I'll ask myself then.
I'll likely be wondering whether the color code
Now universal at stoplights—green, amber, red—
Though a mere convention, may suggest a unity
Beneath the endless diversity of our species.
Maybe unity will prove my recurring theme
When I master the art of meditation,
Beginning with the unity of the varied stories
Told at the table of my host this evening
That I won't be hearing and their kinship
With stories I'll hear at tables elsewhere
Where I happen to be a guest some other day.

Love and Duty

Though I'd rather receive a favor
Prompted by love than a favor
Prompted by duty, I'm grateful for duty
When love isn't available.
The moist loaf of banana bread
A neighbor brought me last month
When my arm, still healing from a fall,
Made kitchen work a challenge
Couldn't have tasted better if love
Had prompted each step of the recipe,
Though then I could have believed
The time she gave to its making
Was more of a pleasure for her than a chore.
But just because her pleasure was less,
Her sense of duty deserves commending,
Duty promptly displayed, not grudging.
And why not admit that pleasure and duty
Are often braided together too tightly
To be distinguished? Are you driving
To the grade school science fair
This Saturday afternoon—
Where your nephew is scheduled
To present his exhibit on tadpoles—
Because you regard the role of uncle
As meaningful or because whatever
Your nephew does delights you?
Are you off to see Aunt Jenny
This Sunday because it's your turn
To drive to the nursing home
Out past the suburbs and she always
Seems glad to see you, or because an hour

With her always lifts your spirits,
Her liveliness in the midst of frailty,
Her questions about your work that require
Specific answers, not generalities?
And then her mentioning she's almost certain
That the county forest she used to love
To hike in can't be much more
Than a five-mile drive away.
She isn't up to going, but you are.
It would do her a world of good
To know that you loved it too.

Second Best

I'd like to believe I was brave enough
To confront the young father at the table near mine
This morning at the health-food restaurant
When I happened to see him slap his son
For spilling a glass of orange juice,
That what held me back was the fear my reproof
Might only make him harder to live with.
But I have to admit that beneath the fear
Of doing more harm than good lay the fear
He might throw his napkin down on the table
And storm out, leaving his son behind,
As if to say, "Big shot, try fathering for yourself."
Only if I were ready to rise to that challenge,
It seemed to me then, could I claim the right
To issue a reprimand, and I saw no evidence
I was ready. I couldn't summon the faith
That once I'd acted I'd discover within me
A well of loving patience I never suspected
This morning when I left the hermitage
Of my quiet side street to visit the world.
All I can do now is fall back on the lesser virtue
Of honesty, along with the virtue of giving
The young father the benefit of the doubt.
Maybe he felt ashamed of himself
Almost at once, while adopting a pose
Of cool indifference. Maybe he swore an oath
To himself only yesterday to impose more discipline
On moods he's inflicted on others for far too long.
And here he is, breaking his oath already
While other fathers like him, whose own fathers
Were just as hotheaded as his father was,

Have taken the first small steps in the right direction,
Learning to count, for instance, slowly to ten.
So why, he wants to know, is the task so far
Proving too hard for him?

A Key

If she didn't worry you'd take it the wrong way,
She might send you the key she found
While cleaning a dresser drawer this morning,
The key to the apartment she shared with you
Many years ago. The wrong way would be
To read the gesture as a confession
That she's grown to miss you, that now she can see
She made a mistake when she decided
She wouldn't be happy enough as the heroine
Of a novel in which you played the part of hero.
The right way to read the key would be
As evidence that among the stories
That when strung together make up her life
You play a central part in one,
One it does her good to recall.

Just imagine how different our country would be
If more people managed to think like her,
How many thousands of keys would be mailed daily
In the hope of bringing joy by assuring
Those who opened the envelopes
That they were remembered fondly still.
Here's proof not merely in words
But in something more solid, more tangible,
Once clutched in the hand, once carried.
Nobody then would ask if the postal service
Was still a necessity. The notion that it should pay
Its own way would be as strange

As asking the same of our public schools,
Our parks, our fire departments, our water towers.

Just when you felt most alone, a key
Might arrive in the mail to prove that the work
Of keeping alive what matters
Isn't so lonely as you've supposed.

Too Bad

Too bad you met me when I was small-hearted and spiteful
And not as I am now, known for my generosity,
Someone who'd never utter the hurtful phrases
Uttered in an earlier era by a man I admit identical
To me in name and in DNA but in nothing else.
Yes, the path from his consciousness
To my own is continuous, but marked by so many changes
In landscape and climate as it winds from a valley floor
Through lowland meadows to mountain freshets
It ought to be thought of as many paths, not one.
Not to answer my letters now seems like blaming a grandson
Bent on reform for the crimes of his granddad.
Isn't it time to turn to the new law
That asks the past to bury itself while the present
Sets sail at sunrise, off to a newfound land?
Do you think I'll tell the natives I happen upon
That they're squatting on land I can prove is mine?
Maybe the man you remember would say such things,
But not the man who's written you all the apologies
I've written since then, which you've answered with silence.
If you merely wanted to be left alone,
You'd have written back once to tell me so.
Silence with you, I'm sorry to say, seems a strategy,
A Siren call to lure me into the past
And leave me lost among reefs and ice floes.
How often must I explain that it isn't working,
How often write you in a voice civil and patient,
Which only you won't accept as mine?

The Right Time

This may be the right time, my friend believes,
Now that his joints have begun to creak,
To work at making his spirit more limber,
Stretching out the kinks, for instance,
In the ligaments used to set grudges aside.
This is the time to remind himself that his parents
Raised him as they believed responsible parents
Would choose to raise him. True, he still wishes
They'd told him more often to be brave
Rather than extra cautious. He still wishes
They had assured him at least once a week
That he was wonderful rather than warning him
That the world didn't owe him anything.
They served the truth as they saw the truth:
Through the cracked window in the rented kitchen
Overlooking the weed-choked alley,
Where it wasn't a good idea for a child to play.
Instead of regretting the time it's taken
To widen the angle of his perspective
As he's searched for a setting more bright and airy,
It's time to wish that he didn't have to fall back
On dreams to tell them not to delay their visit,
To cross over the river now and climb
The wooded hillside to his airy bungalow.
There he is on the porch, waiting to welcome them
In the dusk with lights burning
In every window, and the shades pulled up.

Driving to Syracuse

I'm not obliged to offer a lift
To the young man standing on the shoulder
A hundred yards ahead with his thumb stuck out.
I've made no promise, after all,
Directly or indirectly, to meet him here.
As for the question whether, obliged to or not,
I ought to stop, that depends on whether
I suppose I'll be better off pretending
That this stranger was in fact a friend.
And if I do suppose it, the question remains
Whether now is the time to show I do.
Don't I have a duty more pressing to use
The three-hour drive to Syracuse as I've intended:
To enlarge the remarks I'm to make this evening
At my late friend's memorial service?
Instead of merely listing his many virtues,
I should tell a story to show a few in action,
A story presented with the vividness and the wit
That my friend would have been delighted by.
No doubt he'd have accepted my reasons for stopping
And then for feeling obliged to make conversation.
But this is no time to turn to my friend for sympathy.
It's time to help him by leaving my listeners
With a sharper sense of his uniqueness,
So they can bring him to mind more vividly
In the years still left them. Of course, if I leave the speech
Just as it is, it's possible when I rise to give it
I'll be inspired by a flow of eloquence
Not available to methodical preparation.
But a plan ought not to be based on a faith in miracles.
Better the faith that somebody else

Driving this afternoon to Syracuse will offer
The young man the ride that I haven't offered,
Somebody looking for company with the living only,
Not with the living and the dead.

III

First Mate

I don't want to limit myself to history,
Don't want to deny myself the liberty
Of contemplating what didn't happen
But might have if the first mate, say,
On Columbus's flagship, the *Santa María,*
Had tried his best, as a man of peace,
To persuade his captain that their enterprise
Might profit more from trading with the natives
Than from seizing their land and making them slaves.

Would Columbus have been open-minded
Enough to give this argument a fair hearing,
Along with the argument that it would be easier
To convert the natives if they were trading partners,
Not property? The odds, I admit, are against it,
Given that his virtues were those of an explorer—
Courage and confidence—not justice, not sympathy.

Long odds, but not impossible odds,
Despite his reluctance to accept advice
From a subordinate, if the mate,
Appealing to his captain's hankering
To appear in the eyes of the world
Magnanimous as well as masterful,
Had promised to keep his own part
In revising the policy of his superior
A secret.

No monuments, then, in this alternative history,
Would have praised the mate for his deep humanity.
All would have praised the captain, who alone,

Or almost alone, would have known the truth:
That if his mate had been a yes-man,
Not a hero, the logbooks and charts
Would be smeared with blood.

We

I'm gratified by the use of the word *we*
In the sentence my neighbor utters quietly
As she stands in her driveway, in her yellow raincoat—
"We really needed this rain"—
A *we* that includes not only a gray-haired white man
And a black woman whose hair is still dark but also
Some of the green life we've gathered about us:
The pin oaks and silver maples, the holly
And lilac and dogwood, whose ancestors
Did what they could to make a home here
Millions of years before our ancestors
Walked down the gangway of a steamer from Bremen
Or were led in chains from a sailing ship
That had left Sierra Leone two months before.
We needed this rain to remind us we don't dwell
In a desert we have to cross to reach a promised land.
Here we are in the land of promises
Kept and not kept that we've promised ourselves
To be concerned with. Look how these trees
Are concerning themselves with the rain
That the grass is already welcoming
With many shades of a deeper green.

New Light Tabernacle

I'd be willing to drive an extra ten minutes to shop
At a grocery store unplugged from the grid,
Its lights and heating provided by solar panels,
Though I admit that an extra thirty minutes
Might prove a problem. I have my own life to live,
After all, which requires keeping the friendships
That matter to me in good repair
While saving an hour or two, now and then,
For writing to the editor of my local paper
A temperate letter on the injury done the earth
By an extra degree of global warming,
Making the obvious point that bears repeating
Without the indignation that offends more readers
Than it persuades. Still, I don't want to deny
That the few willing to drive the whole half hour
May also have a list of priorities
That it costs them dearly to put on hold.
What for me is an optional extra
Is for them a commandment they must obey.
The world would be far smaller and shabbier
Without its saints, without the zealots
Who can't be content with halfway measures.
I hope I never dismiss as melodramatic the few
Who chain themselves to the fence of a power plant
Where the turbines are turned by burning coal.
I hope I never mock as inconsistent the few
Who, having sold their cars to promote clean air,
Hitch a ride with a friend to attend a protest.
The moderate many in biblical times
Who didn't give all they had to the poor
And follow their footloose prophet when invited to

Didn't look down their noses at those who did.
They admired them for thirsting after perfection
As I admire those who are thirsting now.
Of course, I don't agree with the zealots who argue
No fellowship can exist between friends of the earth
And those who believe a better world awaits us
Beyond the earth. We can make them our allies,
I argue, if we dwell on their faith that one day
In seven should be set aside to commemorate
The earth's creation, that the commandment to rest
Applies to beasts of burden as well as to humans.
And maybe I'll tell the zealots an anecdote
That shows how I owe my arriving on time
At a meeting in Pittsburgh on the dangers of fracking
To the ministry of the New Light Tabernacle,
How when I stopped in the rain on a lonely byroad
To fix a flat with a jack I discovered missing,
The only car that pulled in behind mine
Displayed on its bumper, in radiant letters,
The two-word announcement "Born Again."
Did I tell the driver, when he offered to help,
That I thought one birth was enough for anyone?
No, I accepted his offer gladly, and gladly listened,
While he changed my tire, to the story of his conversion:
How one Sunday morning, already drunk,
Worried he'd glimpsed a squad car in his rearview mirror,
He swerved into the crowded lot of a church
And scooted inside, only to find himself
Listening to a sermon that asked the question,
Are you living the life you want to live?
No, he wasn't, and the rest is history.

So he explained while bolting my spare on,
Cheerful, though soaked to the skin, impervious.
And who was I, as I watched him, to doubt
That he'd not only tried to change but had succeeded,
That the new man was not the old?

Beyond Will

The question whether faith alone,
If it's pure enough, can move a mountain
May still be open, but it's a fact that the will
Can't do it, the will that without the help of the body
Can't even move a desk chair a little closer
To the desk where you're planning to write
Another letter to your congressman
Explaining why a vote for the carbon tax,
However hard it may fall on the coal town
In the midst of his district, will help the planet.

By an effort of will you can make your arguments
More powerful than you made them before,
But you can't will him to be persuaded,
To give more weight to the future of life
On earth than he gives to his own future
In the party that he belongs to, to winning
Another term on Election Day.

Something other than argument is required
For a change like that, some conversion experience
That makes being an earthling more important
Than being the kind of patriot he's always been.
How likely is that, do you suppose—
The chance that he'll have a vision or dream
In which the ghost of the friend he admired the most
Stands at the end of his bed to tell him
It's now or never to repair our climate?

When the vision ends, he'll rub his eyes
And look about him, poised on the edge of belief

But faltering. Then all that's needed is the accident
Of your letter arriving that very morning.
Yesterday he would have read it as addressed
To extremists only, not to the calm and thoughtful.
But today, a day of wonders, it's addressed to him.

Thought Experiment

I believe I can say with Socrates that I'd rather
Be thought a bad man while in fact a good one
Than be thought a good man while in fact a bad.
But I can't be certain I'd be strong enough
To persist in my choice without one friend
I could share the truth with, that I'd be secure
With no one but me in my audience,
Urging me on. Granted, I'd have an easier time
Than a younger man who made the same choice,
Since I'd have only a few years left to persist
In a life without company. I'd be more likely
Than he would be to give over the thankless task
Of persuading those impervious to all evidence,
Turning instead to the tasks I could do alone
At home, like feeding the sickly plants
In my yard with extra compost or writing
Fundraising letters, under an alias,
For a program in wetland conservancy.
A younger man might look for succor
In the thought of a time to come, however distant,
When his name would be cleared of suspicion.
But I'd be inclined—when I needed support
More personal than the teachings of Socrates—
To seek comfort by turning to friends of mine
No longer among the living, familiar shadows
Who I'm confident would refuse to join the crowd.
"Be with me now, for a while, beloved ghosts,"
I would call to them, and they would answer,
If allowed to answer, "Here we are."

Dependence Day

Though the Fourth of July deserves the parades,
Speeches, and fireworks that commemorate
The declaration of our independence
From the country we left behind us,
What about adding a holiday in early spring
With a focus more global that honors dependence
In all its varieties, beginning with the dependence
Of the animal kingdom on the kingdom of plants,
And the dependence of both on the minerals
They're composed of, the elements left behind
After a star, having exhausted its fuel,
Fell in on itself and exploded. Here we are,
On a planet composed of stellar debris,
Alive together in a spacious cosmos—
That's the theme of our holiday as we pause
To acknowledge our debt to our providers.
Dear brotherly spear of grass, pushing up
From a bed of star ash, we salute you
For making the oxygen we depend on.
Dear sister cow, browsing the grass in a field
South of San Antonio on this fine April morning,
It's your milk, we're glad to proclaim,
That's provided the slices of cheese for the sandwiches
In the lunch boxes of the farmer's children,
Rosemary and Travis, as they ride the bus
To the high school on Dependence Day.
Today every class, no matter the subject,
Will try to widen the usual frame of reference,
Including the health class taught by the school nurse,
Mrs. Deronda. Students, on other days
When we've talked about microbes, we've viewed them

Primarily as invaders. But today we want to acknowledge
That clusters of them—far more numerous than the stars
Visible on a clear night beyond the town glare—
Are busy within us, protecting and nourishing.
On other days, when discussing addiction, we've focused
On the damage that drugs can do to our bodies.
But today we'll be dealing with the damage
They're doing in cities south of the border
To people who won't cooperate with the drug lords,
Who have to leave home to save themselves.
Today we'll be looking at photographs of families
Camped on the Rio Grande, longing to cross
Into our country and begin again.
It's obvious how they depend on us.
But today let's focus on our dependence on them,
How only through them can we be the people
We want to become, the fabled welcomers
Of the huddled and homeless, ever loyal
To the hopeful republic that once proved willing,
Though we brought few assets
We could identify, to let us in.

Three Pages

In the history of my country as yet unwritten,
The woman who fell from the deck of the *Mayflower*
As it rode at anchor off the shore of the New World
Gets more than the single sentence
William Bradford allows her in his narrative
Of Plymouth Plantation. I can understand
Why he wouldn't have lingered on her even though—
As a note in my edition informs me—she happened
To be his wife. His book, after all, is about
The community he helped to lead, not about himself.
I can understand why he didn't mention the fact
That the woman—the note also informs me—
May have cast herself in the water. His book, after all,
Is about the triumph of hope over adversity
With the aid of divine assistance, not about despair.
All the more reason to give her at least a page
In the history of the country as yet unwritten
That tries to imagine what she must have suffered
When saying good-bye to many dear ones
Not to be seen again. And how lonely she felt
When crossing the sea with people who considered
The waves of grief that swept over her
As evidence of ingratitude for the promised land
Waiting for them at the end of the voyage.
And then to arrive at last at the edge of a wilderness
Where no one was waiting to welcome them,
No hearth fire where they could assure themselves
That the worst was at last behind them.

And beside this extra page, there's room in the history
As yet unwritten for a page on the granddaughter

Of the woman's niece, whose letter to a cousin in Boston,
Unearthed only recently, describes her efforts
To persuade her husband not to join the wagon train
About to roll west. Why can't we stay here,
She wants to know, here where our parents
Made a good life, worshipping as they pleased?
Why must we leave the land grown dear to us
For the sake of a few more inches of topsoil
And fewer stones to be hauled from fields
To make plowing easier? A page that dwells
On her effort, when overruled, to set aside
Resentment and move on. And decades later,
When their children ask them what they remember
Most vividly from their westward trek, the account includes
Not only her seconding of her husband's story
Of the sight from a hill, near sundown,
Of the green dell they were destined to farm,
But a page describing what she doesn't mention:
Their wagon's passing, one rainy morning,
In the middle of nowhere, a makeshift grave
With its wooden cross already listing
And no one to clear the weeds away.

Children's Day

We love our children as much as the people of Troy
Loved theirs, people who realized,
By the ninth year of the siege, that time
Was working against them, that they could make sure
Their children wouldn't be sold into slavery
Only if they were willing to give back Helen,
As the Achaeans demanded, with all her treasure.

The only argument against it was that Trojan honor
Might be sullied by the admission that many had died
In a cause finally not worth the sacrifice.
It hurt their pride too much to admit it,
As it hurts our pride too much to acknowledge
That we haven't protected the planet under our protection,
The one to be inherited by the children
Whose efforts in crayon festoon our kitchens.

We have to hope it isn't too late
To change our habits enough so Earth Day
Comes to feature the children of every town on earth
Parading down the local equivalent of Elm Street
Or Main Street crowned with laurel or ivy
And bedecked with flowers they plucked themselves
From the gardens they tend behind their schools.

We have to hope such festivities are more likely
Than the one in Troy that honors the anniversary
Of the day when the siege was finally lifted.
Imagine the Trojan children bedecked with flowers
Dancing down streets never burned to sing in the agora
How once, long ago, Hector the brave led the embassy
That ushered Helen with dignity to the ships.

IV

Rare Mood

It's more than a little daunting
To conclude we're not, after all,
The handiwork of a god,
Just a late descendant of pond scum.
Still, we can take some pride
In having written all the bibles ourselves,
Each with a prophet or two
Who's more than a little vexed
With our neglecting again
The welfare of those outside
The walls of our family compound,
With our failure to clothe the naked
And feed the hungry.
We can take some pride in allowing
A rare mood of concern for others
To outweigh, on a page of scripture,
A host of moods more self-absorbed.
It's heartening to read how a father—
Home after a day when he's failed
To sell one plowshare or pruning hook
To the farmers who shop in Jericho—
Tries not to reprove his daughter
For setting her chores aside
To draw water for strangers—
Servants as well as masters—
And for all their camels, though at first
He's tempted to shout, "How long
Do you think our well will support us
If you forget that among the virtues
Thrift should be listed first?"
And if he shouts it, that very night

A voice in his dream reminds him
His daughter is a blessing, not a burden.
What can he do, he wonders,
To make sure that the husband
He helps her choose, however pious,
However many his virtues,
Understands he's a lucky man?

A Daughter of the Puritans

She can't deny that the lives of her forebears
Possessed a drama her life is missing,
A drama intrinsic to their conviction
That they were born not only to life on earth
But to woe or bliss everlasting.

On many nights they studied their own journals,
Asking themselves if the entries revealed
The thoughts of the lost or the thoughts of the saved.
What if the good works they considered listing
Were only clumsy attempts to compensate
For a lack of the requisite hope and faith?

Less drama for her but less worry as well
If the chance for some other life is denied her.
In that case her only task is to dwell on earth
In a manner she's not ashamed of.
More time and reason to concern herself
With the lives of the last and least,
Now that the promise made them of quick promotion
In another kingdom has been withdrawn.

And now that the world she inhabits
Isn't a bridge to a better one, she's inclined
To note in her journal that this Tuesday evening
Is the first warm evening of spring
And she doesn't know how many springs
Are still left her, though she's concluded

The number left to her soul will be the same
As the number left to her body.

And now she's adding a note about the moon
Outside her window, how it doesn't look pale tonight
With longing for the fire the sun possesses.
It looks glad to be passing along the light it's receiving,
Providing the dark with a little texture,
The weft of moonlight falling on open ground
And the warp of shadow.

Questions for Lazarus

I've been waiting a long time, Lazarus,
In this little park across from your house
Here in a hamlet in Roman Palestine,
For you to send out a message
Saying the shock of returning to life
From the region beyond it has waned a little
And you're willing at last to grant an interview.

By now you must realize I'm not interested
In getting a scoop for my paper,
That I'm acting as an agent for those with a pressing
Practical need to learn what they can
About the zone they will soon be entering.
Who else can I turn to but you, the only person
I know who's returned from the famous bourn
From which no traveler ever returns
Except in myth, and then only rarely?

Think back, Lazarus, to your ignorance
When you set off into the void alone,
And you'll understand why I want to ask
Whether the passage may be compared
To a dreamless sleep or to a dream
Bright enough for you to describe its setting.
If you had some light, did you find yourself
In a garden like this one, with benches
Circling a fountain, or in a desert?

If your dream was dark, and you heard a voice
Calling your name, would you describe it
As eager to answer questions about your past,

Whether, say, the life that you lived on earth
Was one of those you were meant to live,
And if not, was there reason for you
To have chosen it anyway? And when you found out
You would have to return to it for a while
Before you'd be allowed to go forward,
Did the voice explain why?

I know you may not be at liberty
To offer specifics, but can you say something
In general about how dying has altered
Your view of life? Would you say, for instance,
You look forward to dying again,
Now that you know what lies beyond it,
Or would you say that once was enough,
That you'd be interested in alternatives,
In outcomes, say, more festive than death
And more sociable, where stillness is only
One option among many, not our fate?

Former Lives

It can lead to the practice of tolerance, the notion
That the soul returns to earth more than once
And remembers at least a few faint glimmers
Of the life just prior to the one at hand.
It can prompt you to be more patient with a friend
Who's linked her fate to the fate of a man
She knows is liable to wander off
Just when she needs him. Better this life,
You'll hear her telling herself, than the dull
Fifty-year marriage she dimly recalls
To a husband too sluggish to go anywhere.

And think how much easier it will be
To put up with the spendthrift cousin of yours,
Who has to borrow from you most months
To pay his mortgage, if you can suppose
He recalls enough of his prior life
As a penny-pincher to make him decide
To err this time on the side of extravagance.
Better by far to be left with nothing, he reasons,
Than to die as he did the last time,
With the shame of an unspent hoard.

As for your cousin's daughter, who plays the cello
As only a few can play it but who limits her audience
To herself and a few close friends,
No need for you to pity her for suffering
From the same self-doubt that may have thwarted
Her mother's career as a performer,
Not if you can suppose she devoted
Her prior life to pleasing crowds

Of concertgoers on every continent
And is eager now for a life more private.

At last to focus on playing each piece
As she believes the composer would want to hear it.
How refreshing, it seems to her,
And how challenging, after playing for thousands,
To play for one.

Nobody Knows

Nobody knows why our fate was different
From the fate of our intelligent cousins,
The Neanderthals and Denisovans,
Who left Africa for Europe and Asia
Long before we did, and when we followed,
Lived near enough to us for some interbreeding
Over many millennia before they vanished
From the fossil record. Maybe one of their genes
Made them susceptible to a pathogen
That our genes managed to hold at bay.
Or maybe their language skills were less developed,
The tenses not yet distinguished, and no subjunctive
For handling hypothetical situations
As opposed to those in the here and now,
Making it harder for them to plan a hunt.
No way to talk about what might go wrong,
How to shift, if required, from plan A to plan B.
Or else their temperament was more rational,
Leading them to conclude, when their prayers
In times of famine went unanswered,
That the gods, if they existed, weren't interested
In the plight of mortals. So they were prone
To succumb more often to loneliness and despair,
While we—preferring daydreams to facts whenever
Facts seemed to work against us—assumed
That the gods would listen if we praised them
Often enough and reminded them of their wish
To be known to favor justice as opposed to whim.
It didn't take long for us to suppose that in hard times
We were still dear to the gods who mattered,
Though they sometimes relied on agencies

To distribute their gifts that proved understaffed
For reasons not clear to us, so we had to be patient.
It was easy for us, though not for our cousins,
The no-nonsense Neanderthals and Denisovans,
To imagine the messenger sent to relieve us
Caught in a snowstorm and forced to shelter
In a cave for a while. Easy for us to picture her
Warming her icy wings by a fire of twigs
While singing a hymn to keep up her spirits.
If she could suffer like this for us, we agreed,
The least we could do was to give her time.

Palmyra

Those who would rather die than disavow
The gods they worship deserve an entry
In a book of martyrs. But so does someone
Like the museum director who wouldn't flee
His beloved Palmyra when the zealots of ISIS
Were closing in. He stayed behind
To attempt the impossible: to persuade the victors
That every form of worship deserves defending
Against the enemy of them all: obliteration.

Believers won't think of him as a martyr
Because he regarded none of the temples
He tried to save as the house of a living god.
And nonbelievers will tend to suspect him
Of having a favorite among the many
Various gods under his protection:
Sun gods and earth gods, gods quick to anger
And gods with an endless supply of patience.

All the more reason for my friends and me
To lift a glass on his birthday
To the spirit of a faithful non-redeemer
Who wouldn't abandon the temples
Empty for centuries, who cherished them
Because they were cherished long ago.

"Now we are few," we'll acknowledge,
"But one day, if we succeed in describing
How he served the goddess of memory,
Mother of the Muses, as she deserves
To be served, we'll be many more."

The Fall of Man

Though the doctrine that man is fallen explains
Why so much human behavior is disappointing,
It doesn't explain why my real estate agent
Steered me away from the mansion that caught my eye,
With its fat commission for him,
To the plain-faced bungalow that fit my budget.

And though it explains why I think so little
About the people who suffer injustice
I'm not likely to suffer—those, for instance,
Held without trial for years in prisons
Around the world—it doesn't explain
Why the reporter who's been denied permission
To visit even one prison has written a book
That includes dozens of interviews with survivors.

If she's just as fallen as I am, she's been granted
Some kind of reprieve I haven't been granted,
Though after I read her book I dreamed one night
I'd joined a fleet of rowboats setting out before dawn
From the Florida Keys to convince the guards
In our offshore prison that they had more choices
Than fallen creatures are thought to have.

I knew I was dreaming when a guard,
Still in pajamas, went scurrying barefoot
Down a corridor to unlock a cell door
And explain to the startled occupants how a fog

Inside him that he'd always assumed
Part of the coastline had suddenly lifted.

Even in my dream I remember wishing
They'd hurry to make their getaway
Before the fog blew in again.

At Chartres

It's more than a place to shelter from the rain
While listening to a sermon about forgiveness.
No need of a grand building of stone for that,
Of fluted pillars rising more than a hundred feet
To a vaulted ceiling. No need of windows
That instead of providing a view of the town
And the farms beyond, the barns and orchards,
Display in colored glass the faces of saints and angels.
Here is a church that offers its congregation
Not merely talk of the New Jerusalem
But an actual portal or anteroom.
Here is a chance for believers to feel
Something akin to the awe that's waiting
Once they pass through to the other side.

But if there's no gate that the church can open,
No Jerusalem beyond the gate, only oblivion,
Does that mean a cathedral has to be visited
As a castle nobody lives in now is visited
By students of life in the Middle Ages?
Does it mean its purpose should be reconceived
As an abandoned mill might be reconceived
To serve as affordable housing or as a clinic
Or a civic center? Wouldn't that be boorish,
Like using a painting as a piece of canvas
To patch a chair with, like using
A marble statue as a coatrack?

So what's the alternative that requires
No alterations, that welcomes the solemn feelings
Summoned by this cavernous vaulted space?

Can I imagine a congregation of urban planners
From around the world filling the pews
On weekends to muse on the possibility
Of building the New Jerusalem on earth,
An earth made green again, as Blake imagines?
Can I see Chartres as the headquarters of a practical
Pilot program for asking what features
Would any design for a city want to include
So would-be residents could live in harmony?

Even if I assume that each participant
Will be filled with the awe that Chartres
Often induces, free for the moment
Of the pride that insists on domineering,
It's hard for me to believe that their joy
Of fellowship in a single enterprise
Will succeed in bridging their differences,
However sincere their attempts at compromise.

Still, if they need a miracle to keep talking,
It needn't be a grand one. A small one might do.
One of the planners might claim to hear the walls
Of the church speaking to him directly,
Assuring him that long ago their design,
Like the design being debated now,
Was only a sketch on paper,
Subject to last-minute changes and long delays
That caused the masons and carpenters

Who'd said they were ready to start at once
To begin to lose interest and drift away.

And then another planner may claim that the walls
Have prophesied to her in a dream
That however late in the day the laborers
In the New Jerusalem take up their tasks,
They won't be too late to contribute something
Before passing the task along
To those who are waiting to move it forward,
Glad that the project has no end.

V

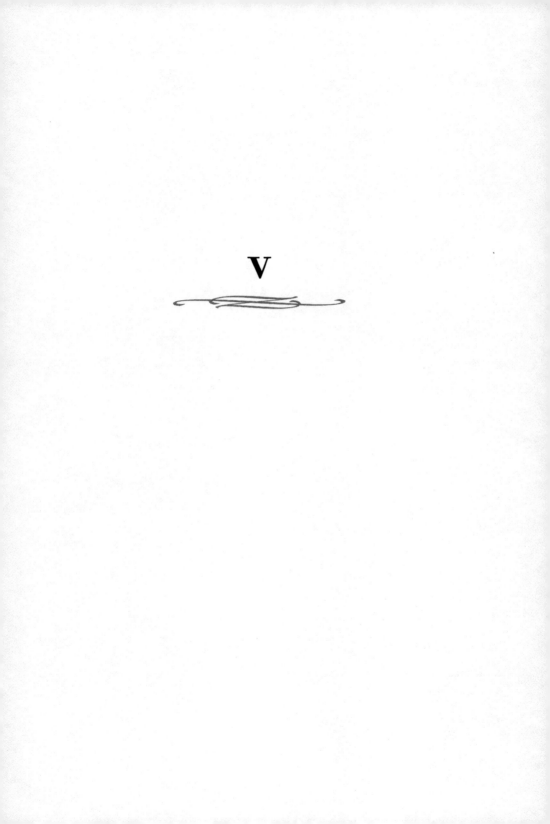

Art and Life

It's no surprise that in fiction the central figures
Tend to learn more by the end than people
Commonly learn in the actual world,
Where many keep making the same mistakes.

Novelists start with their own experience,
Which includes going to bed convinced
That their current project is almost finished,
Only to find, in the candid light of morning,
That it still needs many more months of work.
What better proof that learning goes on
Even in sleep, that one's sense of fitness
Grows in the night like corn or bamboo?

Is the newest version truer to life
Or simply more shapely, more charming?
Sometimes it's hard to tell.
The hero before was recognizable,
A man, say, liable to fritter away his life
In random pastimes. But now he does more
To resist his temperament, so readers,
Instead of looking down from on high,
May be willing to stand in his shoes awhile.

As for the heroine, the revision suggests
She still is a woman who hides,
Beneath her apparent warmth, a seam of coldness.
But now the coldness conceals a wound
That makes trust a challenge.
Now she wants to know where her courage

Is supposed to come from
If she can't find it when she looks within.

The more they learn, the truer they are in spirit
To the fact that every draft of the novel
Is another chapter in the single story
Slowly unfolding in which the author
Learns by trial and error what the work
Needs more of to be complete.

In the meantime, it's clear that the hero's remorse
Near the end of the manuscript for the grief
His want of direction has caused the heroine
Is more convincing than it's ever been.
Instead of giving a speech that seems
Too polished to be spontaneous,
He seems to be groping for words, not sure
What he'll say until he says it, and then
Not sure if he ought to be satisfied
Or open to one more try.

Simon Pell

When somebody asked Simon Pell,
The leader of the first workshop
I wanted to be a part of, if writing a poem
Could be compared to a voyage of discovery,
He said he thought the figure too grand,
A fancy way of saying it's often hard
To tell where your poem is headed
Until you get there and look around.

Simon Pell, old traveler among books,
Who said, when one of us asked
If a poem had to be true to the facts of history,
That being true to the probable was close enough,
The probable on a lucky day
When you're more observant than usual
And more open to something unexpected.

As for changing your mind in the midst of a poem,
It only worked, he thought, when you discovered
The subject to be more significant than it seemed at first,
More worth your investigation, not less,
So your readers don't feel you've wasted their time.

Such rules were based on experience, which meant
He had found them useful much of the time,
Though not always. No way to be sure
In advance whether breaking one
Will help a poem, though after you break it,
He added, the answer ought to be obvious.

This was one of the lessons that Simon Pell
Told us he'd learned in the "Somehow School"

Of writing that he belonged to.
According to all the rules, the poem
Under discussion this evening
Can't work, yet somehow it does.
So let's stop a moment to ask why.

The Muse of Music

If I speak of the Muse of Music, it's not to pretend
To believe in a dead mythology but to try to explain
The difference between saying my brother Robert
Wrote music every morning from his late youth
Into deep old age because he enjoyed it
And saying he felt that music was all-important,
That living well meant bringing its beauty
Into his life, meant serving the enterprise
Blessed by its unseen sponsor, the Muse.
For her he skimped in grade school on lunches
To save up for another recording, on seventy-eights,
Of the trios, quartets, and symphonies of the great composers.
For her in high school he disregarded completely
The big concern of his age group—fitting in—
To devote his free time to being inspired
By her truest followers. If you ask me
Whether I think the Muse returned his devotion,
I can answer that the chorus of seven singers
He wrote many songs for, over many decades,
Believed she did, and the cast for his musical.
And I can add that he never spoke of his service
To her as a chore, though early on he was homesick
After he went away to study composing
At the music college our father didn't believe
Could make him employable. If the Muse was watching
When the family drove out to meet the plane
Bringing him home for summer vacation,
She must have cherished him even more
After noting our dapper father's disappointment
With his son's appearance. There he was,
Stepping down the ramp with his long hair

Not combed even once, it appeared, since Thanksgiving,
With a sport coat that seemed to have doubled as a pillow
And shoes scuffed past the help of any polish,
An ensemble that told the Goddess plainly
He only had eyes for her.

Unanswered Letter

I never answered the letter sent me
More than fifty years ago by an editor
Who took it upon himself to explain
Why he had to reject the poems I'd sent his journal,
A letter listing the many instances
Of mannered diction and runaway metaphor.

Two typed pages, single-spaced,
That now seem incredible, knowing as I do
That if he gave every packet no better than mine
The same attention, he couldn't have lasted
More than a month at his job without collapsing,
Unless he needed just an hour of sleep each night.

Two pages, though he may have surmised
How unlikely it was I'd write to thank him,
How easily I'd dismiss his critique
As just what might be expected when a work
Of youthful genius like mine encountered
A timid gatekeeper of the status quo.

However relieved he was when he left his post,
I hope he never thought of the work as useless,
That he always mentioned it in the vita
He sent around to prospective employers
As someone might mention a stint of service
Fighting wildfires in our national forests,

Risking his life for the public good. And I hope
He believed that a few who never wrote back
Might end up writing a poem like this one,

Thanking him in absentia for fighting awhile
At an outpost of beauty in danger at any moment
Of being surrounded and overrun.

Snowplow Driver

"This will make a good story one day"
Is sometimes the only thought that keeps me
From wishing a particular day never happened.
On the one hand, the thought—when my car
Slides off the road on a patch of ice,
Clips a tree, and buries itself in a snowbank—
That I can't afford the repairs. On the other,
The conviction I can turn it into a story
If I'm not afraid of looking ridiculous.
It could make a point as simple as the need
To slow down on a snowy night
When nearing a curve. Or I might dwell
On the anger that often follows a close call
When we think of the gods as amused to observe
Humans behaving as if the errands they're on
Are too momentous for a moment's delay.
There I am in my story, so indignant at happenstance
That I can't sit in my car and wait for the plow.
I have to step out and pace in the snow,
Cursing and shivering. The story might end there,
Or might end with my calming myself with the thought
It wouldn't be fair to blame the snowplow driver
For my predicament. Or else I might wonder
About the story he'll tell later that evening
If his wife is still up when he gets home.
I can see her now, listening at the kitchen table
In her snowflake pajamas and smiling,
Despite her sleepiness, as he claims,
While he pulls his boots off, that he can tell,
Before the stranded say anything, which ones
Will exclaim how glad they are to see him
And which will ask him, "Where
Have you been all night? What took so long?"

War and Peace

In 1949, when I was ten,
A year after the airlift for beleaguered Berlin
Had foiled Stalin's attempt to starve it
And the Marshall Plan was offering battered Europe
A hand to get on its feet, my brother Robert,
Six years older, inched his way, in the room we shared,
Through the thousand pages of *War and Peace*
While I lay sleeping. It took him four months,
An hour a night, a project that seemed to me
Even more peculiar than his listening after school
To symphonies and quartets. Yes, our mother
Had often mentioned the book as her father's favorite,
The one he'd first read, in his village near Uman,
In Tolstoy's Russian, though he'd learned his Russian
After Yiddish and Ukrainian. But that didn't explain
My brother's pressing on after the first few pages.
Four months just to learn about the families
He tried to describe to me, the Bolkonskys
And Rostovs and Bezukhovs, or about the French
Under Napoleon on the march near Moscow,
And Tsar Alexander. It was all so far
From the suburb of St. Louis where we were living
With our peaceable parents, in a quiet neighborhood.
Of course, by the time my brother read Tolstoy
He'd listened to music composed in Madrid and Naples,
In Leipzig, Vienna, and St. Petersburg.
On a Saturday close to his thirteenth birthday,
Before he was driven off to his Bar Mitzvah,
He lost himself in *The Rite of Spring*.
If I say I followed my brother's lead when sixteen
By reading, all summer long, his dog-eared copy

Of *War and Peace*—the Maude translation—
I don't equate my motive for sticking with it—
Wanting to be like him, not left behind—
With his simple wish to open his life
To the wonders available. When I need to list
The wonders I've seen, I begin by returning
To the year I was ten, 1949,
The year that NATO began its efforts
To defend the free world from the world of darkness,
When my brother crossed the border each night
As if darkness were not an obstacle,
As if the iron curtain were a curtain of gauze
No harder to lift than to turn a page.

Violin

It may not be a cure for loneliness,
Devoting your idle hours to learning to play one,
But it's a step in the right direction.
No more resentful daydreams about acquaintances
Whose inner circle of friends was closed to you.
No more useless remorse about being too slow
To reply to all the voices you've recognized
On your message machine. You'll have your hands full
Confronting the immediate challenge of wooden fingers
And squeaky strings. Slowly, over months,
By fits and starts, you'll proceed from the stage
Of raw beginner to advanced beginner
Who can make a familiar tune recognizable,
Playing it through each time with fewer mistakes.
Even if you never progress to playing with others,
You'll earn the right to imagine yourself included
In a band of anonymous folk musicians who've welcomed
As best they can the songs and dances
Tradition has passed to them. You will almost
Feel those others beside you, resting their chins
On their chin rests just as you're doing,
Fretting the strings with one hand while lightly
Using the other to draw the bow.
If you keep at it, the instrument
Will seem an obliging partner who's willing
To play along whenever you feel like practicing,
Glad to repeat a phrase till you master it
And to take a break whenever you need one.
And if, while shut in its case, it daydreams
Of the few who played it before it came
Into your possession, you won't consider them rivals.
You'll feel beholden to them for welcoming

Into their families the guest you're welcoming,
For bestowing upon it the care you're bestowing.
And if their company still isn't enough to satisfy
Your craving for fellowship, think of the people
Destined to play it after it leaves your hands.
It's not impossible that one of them
May consider making the violin his profession.
And if he has second thoughts after a year,
Maybe his sister will take it up and decide
The violin is her destiny. Of course her teacher,
After six years of lessons, may match her up
With an instrument that's been played over centuries
By a score of professionals. But that doesn't mean
Your violin won't have a special place in her heart
As the one she loved first. If she passes it on
To a beginner, she'll encourage the student
To think of the earliest owners of her instrument
With special consideration, how they lived in an era
When music had yet to receive the recognition
It would come to count on. They never dreamed
That every county across the land would one day
Sponsor a band or orchestra, and many factories
And many prisons. And just as you dream the scene
Of the teacher's exhorting her student, so you can dream
The scene of the inmate's signing the schedule
For an hour of practice in the practice room
That's always open. If a general lockdown
Keeps him confined that day, he'll write a letter
Asking the warden for an extra hour of practice
On next week's schedule. And if his appeal
Receives no answer, he'll write again.

For Tony Hoagland

All that's obvious now is how much light
You've taken with you into the dark,
My lively, spirited, truth-telling friend.
But in time, if time is with me,
I'll be glad for every episode
I manage to pull from the dark,
Every proof that I bring you with me.

Now it will be a chore to attend your memorial.
I don't need the memories of your other friends
To round out my own, others all laboring
Under the sad delusion they knew you
As well as I did. But in time,
When this gust of competitive grief blows by,
I'll hear you saying, *Wait it out, Carlo.*
Soon you'll be glad they want to join the ritual
Of urging each other to remember me.

Now I want to focus only on the give-and-take
Of our private dialogues, not on your poems,
Those monologues and addresses meant for everyone.
But in time, if time is with me, I'll be glad
That so much of your private voice
Is caught in your lines, your quick amusement
And indignation, say, at the newest example
Of swagger our country is prone to.

Then I'll be moved by how willing you were
To recast the failings of your country
As magnified versions of your own failings,
Your own pretensions, own betrayals,

How ready you were to slander yourself
In order to make your speaker a participant
In his country's shame, not a looker-on.
When I think of what I know about America,
I think of kissing my best friend's wife
in the parking lot of the zoo one afternoon,
just over the wall from the lion's cage.

Now I worry about keeping them separate,
The facts, on one hand, and, on the other,
The fictions you made of them, but in time
I hope to be guided by your assurance,
In your late lines as well as late conversations,
That experience is often too profuse
And too luxuriant to be divided neatly
Into separate genres, separate files:
Sometimes I prefer not to untangle it.
I prefer it to remain disorganized,
because it is richer that way
like a certain shrubbery I pass each day on Reba Street.

Tony, I don't know if the knots and tangles
In the strands that your friends are weaving
Mean we're succeeding at making your story and ours
Parts of a single story. But if we're failing,
They may show at least how we're trying
To reach out to you as you pass us,
To do our best not to say good-bye.

VI

A Romance

It would be easier to be kind if we knew
We were members of an ensemble that's destined
To perform the romance we're now performing
Again and again till each has acted
Every part in the plot, high and low, at least once.

Easier for the king to care
About working conditions in the palace scullery
If he knew he was destined, sooner or later,
To take up the role of scullion.

Easier for the woodcutter's youngest son,
Who, after many adventures, kills the dragon
Terrorizing the kingdom and marries the princess,
To be grateful for the help he receives from the ferryman,
The old hunchback who poles him across a river
At flood stage without asking a fee.

How could the youth forget his promise
To send the old man an invitation
As his wedding day finally drew near,
Knowing as he would that one day
He'd be assigned to do the poling,
His bad back aching?

It's only sensible, then, for our prince-to-be
To wait at the palace gate on his wedding day
To lead his friend to a place in the royal pew

For the wedding service and then to assign him
To table one in the banquet room.

But what if next morning the actors are told at breakfast
That owing to conditions beyond control of management
Everyone in the troupe must content himself
From this time forward with playing only
The part assigned him in this performance?

Will the prince turn to his friend and say,
With sincere compassion, "Dear ferryman,
Now that you won't be allowed the opportunity
To kill the dragon and court the princess,
I want you to know that your room last night
Here in the palace is yours whenever you need it"?

Maybe he will, given his good intentions,
Though the question remains how long
He'll reserve the room if every year his memory
Of waiting to play the part of the ferryman
Grows more hazy, and his talent for playing
The part of king becomes more clear.

Embodied

I can see how the distinction between mind
And body is often useful, as between the minds
That thought it a good idea to join the protest
Yesterday in front of the White House
And the bodies exposed to the threat of injury.
But to say that today my mind is in Washington
While my body is here in Buffalo,
Is to ignore the fact that we live together
Here in the same house.

Whenever my body sits in the sunroom,
In the armchair by the window,
As it's doing now, I'm in the chair as well,
Looking up from an article on the protest
To admire what spring has done to my yard,
Then opening the book I've been reading this week
On Shakespeare's London.

Later, out walking, I seldom feel
I'm taking my body for a walk.
I feel my mind and body are walking together,
My body signaling by its pleasure that my mind
Is free to focus as it chooses, now on the White House,
Now on the green phenomena of the neighborhood.

And now I'm free to lose myself in wondering
Why Shakespeare, near the end of his writing life,
Didn't do more to make sure his plays were published

Together in their final versions. Didn't he hope
They'd endure long after his body gave up the ghost?

When I get back from my walk, it's dinnertime.
Not only is my body hungry, but I'm hungry too,
Eager to get dinner started in the roomy kitchen,
Sorry a friend at the protest who hasn't returned yet
Won't be one of my guests. How different I am
From the Hamlet who boasts he could live in a nutshell
And count himself the king of infinite space.
I'll be serving dinner in my roomy dining room.

And if a guest asks how my day went
And I give two answers, they won't be the story
Of how things went for my mind as opposed
To how they went for my body, but the story
Of how they went for the ensemble I am
Compared with how I wish they had gone.

I spent some of the day, for instance,
As one of the mourners who followed Hamlet's body
To the graveyard that's waiting for mine one day,
While wishing I was on my way to his coronation,
To the dancing sure to go on all night as his country
Rejoiced in waking at last from its dark dream.

The Night before Halloween

Last year, on the night before Halloween,
My nephew's daughter decided to be an angel
Assigned to watch over shortsighted Mr. Magoo.
But this year she's decided to be a witch
With a crew of pirates in thrall to her,
Which is fine with her father,
Who's glad to help her shape a pointed hat
And blacken a weathered pair of sneakers.

It's good for her to explore her options,
He reasons. Good to learn early that work
Isn't a matter of one true calling
And many ill-fitting substitutes, that more
Than one kind of work can make a person happy,
And every experiment is a chance to learn.

I can see his point that if she ends up earning
Her living, say, as an officer of the law,
Some prior work as a labor leader may prompt her
To let a peaceful protest continue
Without a permit. If she ends up as a labor leader,
Some prior work as an officer of the law
May prompt her to urge the city workers
Who keep the streets clean to end their slowdown
When the mayor finally agrees to parley.

So maybe her being an angel last year
Will prompt her this year to order her pirates
To focus, when boarding a ship under her spell,
Just on the passengers who look as if the loss

Of half their portable property
Won't matter to them in the long run.

As for who she may want to be next year,
If this year's stint as a witch deepens
Her sense of the dangers that threaten
An innocent like Mr. Magoo,
She may want to be an angel again.

It will be a challenge to help him,
A man who believes he's strolling
A country lane when in fact he's crossing
Main Street in killer traffic. Now for the thrill
Of bringing him home at dusk unscathed.

One Thing Is Needful

Whether I need more humility,
Now that my planet is in serious jeopardy,
Or more presumption, is an open question.
Humility reminds me to think of my species
As a single thread in an intricate tapestry
Of millions of threads. But presumption claims
That when I stand back to contemplate the design,
I'm looking down from a platform above the earth.
I'm noting the hundreds of fires that ranchers
And loggers have set in the Amazon.
I'm numbering all the bald spots below
In the High Sierras as another species of pine
Gives up its ghost, gasping for the colder air
No longer available. Humility reminds me
Our species is here and gone in the blink of an eye.
Presumption insists I'm the only hope,
Along with my cohort, of the world we're busy
Wrecking, that it's up to us to widen the margins
Of the passing moment, that it's time to invest
In the myth of a long-lost Eden and the myth
Of the numberless generations to follow ours
Destined to bless us as preservers, not to scorn us
As destroyers. They can't imagine us now,
Those children to come, but we can imagine them
Returning to grade school after a summer
That bears no resemblance to the Death Valley era
Now predicted. Soon their teachers
Will assign them—without any irony—
The topic of a favorite outdoor adventure.
But first they're going to call the roll.
It's good to see you again, Kabir and Carmen,

Chandrash and Lucy, Mingmei and Fred.
Are you ready for long division and fractions?
Are you ready to find Zanzibar on the map?
Humility will inform you you've much to learn.
Presumption will encourage you to learn early
Many lessons that we learned late.

A Journey

If life is a journey, it may not be easy
Even near the end to say for sure
Whether I lost my way or found it.

On days when it seems I've failed,
I may not be certain where my error lay.
Was the furniture I lugged from the past
So heavy that my rented truck sank in the mud,
So I never made it across the isthmus
Into the promised land of the present?
Or did I bring too little with me
Into a present more empty than advertised,
With no groceries and no farms,
No berry bushes or fig trees?

And on days when it seems I've arrived
Where I hoped to arrive, was it a matter
Of finding one path and sticking to it
Or of trying scores of dead-end shortcuts,
Each one a detour I had to take
Before I could be at ease with the route
I would come in time to recognize as my own?

A failure because I arrived too late
At a life that a real hero would have discovered
Many decades earlier. A success because
The story of my slow progress kept me guessing.
How dull the achievement of a competent hiker
Who completes in two hours a hike
That's supposed to take him about two hours.
How much better to meet with so many

Roadside adventures I didn't anticipate
When I started at sunrise that I was lucky
To finish my hike by dusk.

Sunday with Trees

Tomorrow I may try again to persuade old Mr. Bitner,
Who lives in the blistered eyesore down the block,
That it's time to invest in a little scraping and painting.
If he tells me again that his house is an accurate mirror
Of what he feels about himself—how his best years
Are long behind him—I may suggest that sometimes
Pretending to feel what one doesn't feel
May brighten a mood. Or I'll stress how grateful
All his neighbors will be if he manages to lose himself
Now and then in the effort others are making
To make the block look less abandoned.
But today I don't feel like lecturing anyone on civility.
I feel like taking a walk in the woods, among trees
Civil by nature, which warn each other by pheromones
When insects attack them, which use their roots
To send an infusion of sugars into the roots
Of their ailing neighbors. Lucky for me
All their sharing is done unconsciously
So they can escape any pride in their generosity
That might make their company a burden.

Tomorrow I may try to persuade the young couple
Across the street with three young children
Not to make the move they're considering
To a block with more children. If they're patient,
I'll tell them, more families like theirs
Are bound to move in, drawn by their own
Pioneering spirit. In the meantime,
Their family is making their neighbors feel
They live in the midst of life, not at its margin.
But today, rather than lecture anyone about loyalty,

I want to walk among trees loyal by nature,
Trees impossible to seduce by an offer
Of a site more congenial just a mile away.
All are content to root down where they are.
No wonder the birds, knowing the trees will always
Give them a stable home, feel safe to indulge
Their flightiness. Do they know how lucky they are
That their landlords never ask for a penny in rent?
A question the trees are as far from asking
As they are from asking the birds to sing at least
One song a day to them and to no one else.

Breath

It's humbling to dwell on the need
For taking in a mouthful of air
A dozen times a minute
Whether we want to or not,
Whether the air available blows in
From a mountain meadow or from a swamp.

Still, I'm proud of the deep breaths
That our featured speaker tonight is taking
While she waits to be introduced. Her voice
Mustn't quaver as she exposes the lies
Told about our water and soil and air,
The claims they're as clean as they've ever been.

Though she doesn't believe her words
Will be wafted around the world
On an irresistible tide of spirit,
At least she believes that her audience
Will try to give them a fair hearing
If she can deliver them with authority.

When I think of what can be done
With a single breath, I think of the soloist
In the old recording I own, on seventy-eights,
Of Mozart's oboe concerto, of his sudden
Intake of breath at a silent beat
To fill his lungs for a soaring passage.

I hope our speaker's faith this evening
In the worth of her contribution
Is akin to the faith of the musician

As he sends his theme, finely phrased,
Out through the double reeds.

May it meet with good luck
On its unpredictable journey,
Riding farther than many suppose
A theme can ride on a puff of air.

Mary Richert

CARL DENNIS is the author of thirteen previous works of poetry, as well as a collection of essays, *Poetry as Persuasion*. In 2000 he received the Ruth Lilly Poetry Prize for his contribution to American poetry. His 2001 collection, *Practical Gods*, won the Pulitzer Prize. He lives in Buffalo, New York.

PENGUIN POETS

GAROUS
ABDOLMALEKIAN
*Lean Against
  This Late Hour*

PAIGE ACKERSON-
KIELY
*Dolefully, A Rampart
  Stands*

JOHN ASHBERY
Selected Poems
*Self-Portrait in a Convex
  Mirror*

PAUL BEATTY
Joker, Joker, Deuce

JOSHUA BENNETT
Owed
The Sobbing School

TED BERRIGAN
The Sonnets

LAUREN BERRY
The Lifting Dress

JOE BONOMO
Installations

PHILIP BOOTH
*Lifelines:
  Selected Poems
  1950–1999*
Selves

JIM CARROLL
*Fear of Dreaming:
  The Selected Poems*
Living at the Movies
Void of Course

ALISON HAWTHORNE
DEMING
Genius Loci
Rope
Stairway to Heaven

CARL DENNIS
Another Reason
Callings
Earthborn

*New and Selected Poems
  1974–2004*
Night School
Practical Gods
Ranking the Wishes
Unknown Friends

DIANE DI PRIMA
Loba

STUART DISCHELL
Backwards Days
Dig Safe

STEPHEN DOBYNS
*Velocities: New and Selected
  Poems 1966–1992*

EDWARD DORN
Way More West

HEID E. ERDRICH
Little Big Bully

ROGER FANNING
The Middle Ages

ADAM FOULDS
*The Broken Word:
  An Epic Poem of the
  British Empire in Kenya,
  and the Mau Mau
  Uprising Against It*

CARRIE FOUNTAIN
Burn Lake
Instant Winner
The Life

AMY GERSTLER
Dearest Creature
Ghost Girl
Index of Women
Medicine
Nerve Storm
Scattered at Sea

EUGENE GLORIA
*Drivers at the
  Short-Time Motel*
Hoodlum Birds
My Favorite Warlord
Sightseer in This Killing City

DEBORA GREGER
In Darwin's Room

TERRANCE HAYES
*American Sonnets for
  My Past and Future
  Assassin*
Hip Logic
How to Be Drawn
Lighthead
Wind in a Box

NATHAN HOKS
The Narrow Circle

ROBERT HUNTER
Sentinel and Other Poems

MARY KARR
Viper Rum

WILLIAM KECKLER
Sanskrit of the Body

JACK KEROUAC
Book of Blues
Book of Haikus
Book of Sketches

JOANNA KLINK
Circadian
*Excerpts from
  a Secret Prophecy*
The Nightfields
Raptus

JOANNE KYGER
*As Ever:
  Selected Poems*

ANN LAUTERBACH
Hum
*If in Time: Selected Poems
  1975–2000*
On a Stair
Or to Begin Again
Spell
Under the Sign

CORINNE LEE
Plenty
Pyx

PENGUIN POETS

PHILLIS LEVIN
May Day
Mercury
Mr. Memory &
  Other Poems

PATRICIA LOCKWOOD
Motherland Fatherland
  Homelandsexuals

WILLIAM LOGAN
Rift of Light

J. MICHAEL MARTINEZ
Museum of the Americas

ADRIAN MATEJKA
The Big Smoke
Map to the Stars
Mixology
Somebody Else Sold the
  World

MICHAEL McCLURE
Huge Dreams: San
  Francisco and Beat Poems

ROSE McLARNEY
Forage
Its Day Being Gone

DAVID MELTZER
David's Copy:
  The Selected Poems
  of David Meltzer

TERESA K. MILLER
Borderline Fortune

ROBERT MORGAN
Dark Energy
Terroir

CAROL MUSKE-DUKES
An Octave Above Thunder:
  New and Selected Poems
Red Trousseau
Blue Rose
Twin Cities

ALICE NOTLEY
Certain Magical Acts
Culture of One
The Descent of Alette
Disobedience
For the Ride
In the Pines
Mysteries of Small Houses

WILLIE PERDOMO
The Crazy Bunch
The Essential Hits of Shorty
  Bon Bon

DANIEL POPPICK
Fear of Description

LIA PURPURA
It Shouldn't Have Been
  Beautiful

LAWRENCE RAAB
The History of Forgetting

BARBARA RAS
The Last Skin
One Hidden Stuff

MICHAEL ROBBINS
Alien vs. Predator
The Second Sex
Walkman

PATTIANN ROGERS
Generations
Holy Heathen Rhapsody
Quickening Fields
Wayfare

SAM SAX
Madness

ROBYN SCHIFF
A Woman of Property

WILLIAM STOBB
Absentia
Nervous Systems

TRYFON TOLIDES
An Almost Pure
  Empty Walking

VINCENT TORO
Tertulia

PAUL TRAN
All the Flowers Kneeling

SARAH VAP
Viability

ANNE WALDMAN
Gossamurmur
Kill or Cure
Manatee/Humanity
Trickster Feminism

JAMES WELCH
Riding the Earthboy 40

PHILIP WHALEN
Overtime: Selected Poems

PHILLIP B. WILLIAMS
Mutiny

ROBERT WRIGLEY
Anatomy of Melancholy
  and Other Poems
Beautiful Country
Box
Earthly Meditations:
  New and Selected Poems
Lives of the Animals
Reign of Snakes
The True Account of
  Myself as a Bird

MARK YAKICH
The Importance of Peeling
  Potatoes in Ukraine
Spiritual Exercises
Unrelated Individuals
  Forming a Group Waiting
  to Cross